REFLECTIONS
AT SUNSET

REFLECTIONS AT SUNSET

Juliette Lively Dickey

38-DICK

CONTENTS

MIDDAY
AUTOBIOGRAPHICAL POEMS

SUNSHINE OF GOD'S LOVE INSPIRA-TIONAL POEMS

TWILIGHT REFLECTIONS
BITS AND PIECES

REFLECTIONS AT SUNSET

BY
JULIETTE LIVELY DICKEY
Illustrated by
dickey doodles—lorene dickey

INTRODUCTION

THE DAWNING
OF A POET

ABOUT JULIETTE LIVELY DICKEY

BORN: March 17, 1927 in Burke County, Georgia

PARENTS: James Thaxter and Julia Smith Lively

MARRIED: September 22, 1946 to Benjamin S. Dickey

CHILDREN: Dr. M. Thaxter Dickey, Tampa Florida Professor Florida Christian College Minister, Church of Christ

Dennis Lively Dickey, Trenton, Florida Minister, Church of Christ

Ben S. Dickey, Jr Antioch, CA Training Manager Contra Costa Sheriff 's Dept.

Angie Gifford, Delray Beach, Florida Dispatch Supervisor FAU's Police Dept.

Lorene Dickey, Ocala Florida Florida CDS Staff Assistant

EDUCATION: Waynesboro High School, Waynesboro, Georgia Bessie Tift College, Forsyth, Georgia Continuing Education, CFCC Ocala, Florida

OCCUPATION: Staff Assistant for Florida Dept. Of Revenue Child Support Enforcement, retired.

PUBLICATIONS: Ocala Star Banner, National Library of Poetry in On The Dark Side of The Moon; After The Storm; America at the Millennium; Famous Poets Society, Today's Great Poems; Sparrowgrass Poetry Forum Voices of America and in Florida's Revenue Venue as well as several local magazines.

HOW I GOT STARTED WRITING POETRY

Early one morning in September, Mary, our receptionist came into the office very excited. She worked only twenty hours for us and was teaching an English class at the community college twice a week, also. At college they were studying poetry at the time and a form of unrhymed Japanese, called Haiku. She thought it would be a good idea to compare her young student's writings to the ones we would write in our office. Our office at that time was made up of a myriad of workers. One of them was a high spirited young black girl married to an evangelical minister, another a loud, aged, very opinionated New York Yankee, also a pretty young red neck girl who lived in the forest with her dogs and drove a truck. We had a Cuban mother of two teenagers, a middle aged Don Juan, who thought he was god's gift to women, a short Italian guy who was the world's best optimist and myself—an ethical, no nonsense, white haired grandmother that was raised in rural Georgia and who knew nothing about Japanese haiku. Mary gave us instructions and I was very leery about writing anything. That evening my husband and I were taking our usual evening walk and above us a flock of crows were flying. We had noticed them going out each morning and then coming home again in the evening to roost. The following Haiku just seem to form in my head and I was reluctant to give it to Mary. Finally after much persuasion I did. She liked it and put it in her memo to the office along with several others.

CROWS COME A CAW-CAWING

OVER EACH MORNING

RETURN HOME LATE EACH EVENING

Maybe a month had passed when Mary again approached us to write a poem. This time it was for her Poetry Club that was having a contest. She was insistent and the following is my first attempt at Poetry. Of course, I didn't win the contest but it was fun to try. This in the long run, opened up a new interest for me and an avenue to express my feelings and thoughts.

SPECIAL PEOPLE

I'm Special
Because I'm ME!
Wife, mother, homemaker, secretary, and would-be-poet,
teacher, taxi, caretaker, and always would-be-know-it.

He's Special
Because He's HE!
Husband, father, man of valor, builder, personality true,
talents galore, example of goodness, trustworthy sure!

They're Special
Because they're THEY!
Girls, boys, children, more precious than silver and gold,
in days past brought joy, as days flee more memories unfold.

We are Special
Because we are WE!
We who are older, leaning on a stronger hand,
becoming less bolder and looking forward to the Glory Land!

During the War of Desert Storm, there were many pleas for letters to be sent to the men and women in the Services. I started thinking about how proud I was of my husband, serving in the Army during World War II, and my two sons who joined the navy after High School and served overseas. I wrote "You Are Special" as a tribute to them as well as all those who were in the Service at that time.

YOU ARE SPECIAL

YOU ARE SPECIAL!
You who left your loved ones behind,
to serve on foreign soil for mankind.

YOU ARE SPECIAL!
You who chose to defend this land
to uphold justice and liberty on Arabian Sand.

I ARE SPECIAL!
I chose to serve my Country, just like you,
on foreign soil in World War Two.

THEY ARE SPECIAL!
Two sons on USS ships did sail
on Mediterranean and Red Seas detail.

WE ARE SPECIAL!
Because we believe in Liberty and Justice for all
and pray daily for all of you to return whole.

QUESTIONS

Do you write poetry from inspiration,
Or from much agonizing deliberation?
Does forming the rhymes come easy,
Or do you have to work at being breezy?
Are your thoughts streamline and in order,
Or are they disorganized as flying mortar?
Whichever. . . . . . . it's poetry for sure,
When from the heart it's true!

A lot of my ideas come to me in the middle of a sleepless night. Sometimes I recall events of the day or sometimes I dream of things that are past and sometimes of things to come. I have found that ideas come and go fleetingly if not written down. I have a pen with a light on it to write as the ideas come to me.

AN IDEA

IS

AS
SUBTLE

AS

A cloud drifting in a mild, blue sky,
Or the flutter of a yellow butterfly.
A whisper of a gentle, soft breeze,
Or airy suds that make you sneeze.
The touch of a wild, straying hair,
Or bubbles as they dance in the air.
As lovely as the glow of the moon,
Only to disappear much too soon.

AT NIGHT WHEN I CAN'T SLEEP
INSTEAD OF COUNTING SHEEP
WHEN MY HEAD BEGINS TO CHIME,
MY THOUGHTS TURN TO RHYME.

MIDDAY AUTOBIOGRAPHICAL POEMS

FAMILY ARE SPECIAL PEOPLE

Somewhere early in life I acquired the feeling of being a very special person. This is something I would not trade for all the wealth in the world. It is a very good feeling and takes me though all the bad times in my life with ease. This is a feeling I would like to share with everyone, an assurance of being somebody special whatever the circumstances.

It all started years ago in the backwoods of Georgia with my Dad who was an old man when I was born—a very old grouchy man to others—who always had a kind word for me. He always saw to it I was not pushed aside in the midst of thirteen children. He cared for me and looked after my well being along with that of the other children. I think I am, and have always been, the quietest of all the children in my family.

I remember on the cold winter nights when my dad would come into our unheated bedroom making sure we children were all covered, snug and warm in our beds. I remember him making the older children stand aside and putting me in close to the fireplace to get warm. Little things but big important things to a small child. Even though I was the eighth of thirteen children I was ME—someone special. My feelings were of utmost importance.

When I was a teenager and dating I always had in mind to find that special someone to marry and I did. My husband makes me feel very special and I hope in turn I make him feel that he is the most special person in the world, because he is. He is unique in his way of thinking, and has a way of expressing himself that few others have. He is a very exhilarating person and sometimes explosive but always gentle in his ways of dealing with me or the children. Just being near him to listen to him and enjoy his way of telling things is a thrill. He is never idle but always working at something, always creative and a master at building things. This talent for building he has passed on to his sons. He taught them with patience from their earliest years all phases of the work.

I have tried to pass this feeling of being special along to all of our children, individually, as they are all special to me in their own way. I have never treated them alike as they are not alike in disposition, looks, or intellect. They are very special as individuals to me and to their dad. We have tried to impress upon them that they are special if for no other reason than that they belong to us. They are our offspring and we are special people.

The oldest is special because of his way of digging into books, weightier matters and always studying just for the enjoyment of learning new and challenging things. He has always enjoyed debates and studies to do the best job possible in everything that he undertakes. He enjoys competition and comes out feeling good about his ability even when he has not always won first place.

The second son is special in his own way being entirely different in disposition. He is more of an on-the-spot thinker and doer. He learns from association with people and things, loves people and enjoys mixing and being with others. He encourages others by helping them while he himself may be in need of help at the same time. He is good with children and treats his own as if they are something special.

Our third son is an individual private person. Special in his way of enjoying being by himself more than with other people and keeping his feelings to himself. He, too has a special place for his children but as usual he will not let others see how deeply he cares for them but keeps that private between himself and his children. Sometimes even to the exclusion of his wife. He is a very hard worker and provides well for his family, attends college and does other part time jobs as well as his full time job.

Our oldest daughter is more like her dad in personality with an unusual ability to meet and be at ease with all people, rich, poor, young, old, good or bad with whom she comes in contact. She has a way of making all feel that they too are special people just by talking to her. She has had a variety of jobs and studies that have helped her develop this dynamic personality.

Our youngest child, a daughter, is another special person in her own way with an explosive and volatile personality and her way of defending herself against all people who are older and taller than she. She has a very determined manner about her for one so small in statue. An outdoors girl with a big truck for transportation, but yet she has the ability to draw, paint and is very creative.

All of my family are very special people and I hope that you, too will see the need to encourage each and every child to be a special person in all that they endeavor to undertake. As infants they need that special feeling of belonging. As small children they need this special feeling to become aware of family and friends. As teenagers they need this special feeling to endure all the problems that teenagers face with dating and learning to become more reliable for themselves rather than lean on mom and dad. As adults they need this special feeling to endure all the trials and heartaches that come with living and caring for a family and to have the ability to pass on this very special feeling to other people.

THE 4TH OF JULY

The 4th of July has traditionally been set
for Lively families to meet and 'chew the fat'.
In 1929, eight brothers—Greene, Mark and Jim
Charlie, Fred, Bert, Watson and Kip
along with their sister, Ruth agreed
each year with their families to lead
them to get acquainted with each other
and to know the children of each brother.
When Jim died he left us this little piece of land
where wild flowers and mountain laurel grow in a stand.
It has a swimming hole, a fishing pond, bar-b-que pit
and for visiting a screen pavilion in which to sit.
What a truly great gift he gave to us to share,
so wonderful, we need to really appreciate and care
how we enjoy it and what we leave for others
that will come after us and our brothers.
Louis, Ashton, Evelyn, Q.U., Van, Keely, Hugh Miller,
Juliette, Attalee, Sevena, Octama, Yonce and Katy Bly.
Their families seem to attend and care so much more
than the other cousins who don't often show
for our reunion, time after time, year after year.
They don't seem to realize what is precious and dear. We need to
leave strong traditions for our children
making sure they know how priceless is our freedom,
and the right to walk in this peaceful wooded land
that has to us been handed down from man to man
having first been created by God Above
for us to respect, enjoy and use with love.

A good name and reputation are worth more than silver and gold.

MY LEGACY

My Legacy was handed down
from a man who tilled the ground,
an aged Georgia dirt farmer
who was calm and not an alarmer.

A man who was old before his time
had no hair and was almost blind,
but a sense of humor he did own
along with kids, dogs and home.

No formal education to be had
but plenty of common sense from a lad,
figuring without the benefit of pen or paper
long before computers and the calculator.

He was known for his business cunning
far and near for his fox hunting,
he grew cotton, pine trees and children
loved them all like one in a million.

Never very religious but values true
he handed them down to me for sure,
a legacy worth more than silver or gold
one that withstands and cannot be stole.

He gave me a sense of self worth,
love, and self esteem beginning at birth,
a name of which to be proud
one that stood out in a crowd.

To thirteen the name of Lively he did bequeath,
true, honorable, one in which to have faith,
a legacy that cannot be destroyed by man or beast,
an inward being that will survive most any test.

When confronted with trials and tribulations,
a legacy to hand down to coming generations,
no money or riches did he bequeath,
but a more priceless legacy he gave to me.

On Sunday afternoons my Dad would take all of the children that could walk for a long walk through the woods. He would point out all the interesting flowers, birds, and animal tracks that could be seen. Sometimes it was hard to keep up with him. Later when he couldn't walk very much he would take us riding in the wagon with his old mule hitched to it.

PAUSE AND FEEL THE WIND

Some beautiful memories of long ago,
keep running through my mind in a row,
of a man with a houseful of little kids,
who loved to listen to birds and katydids,
as they walked the woods on Sunday afternoon,
talking, singing or whistling many a tune.

I remember
A gentle Spring day full of blue skies,
when he would point out some special thing to our eyes,
picking beautiful wild flowers and lagging behind
then often pausing to feel the wind.

I remember
a bright lovely balmy Summer day,
when to the swimming pond we headed to play,
following behind a man who like to tease,
pausing every so often to feel the breeze.

I remember
a cool crisp Autumn afternoon
crunching the fallen leaves was a boon,
as together voices, young and old blend,
when we pause to feel the wind.

I remember
On an afternoon in the cold Winter weather,
children crying and laughing together,
as we hurry along in step to his pace,
feeling the cold freezing wind on our face.

THAT OLD MULE JUST PLODDED ALONG

Daddy got us up early at the break of dawn,
To ride down County to the Boyd farm.
He hitched his old mule between the shafts,
While we wolfed breakfast down real fast.
He and Mama climbed up on the spring seat,
With two little kids bundled at their feet.
We four girls scrambled up behind,
With "Giddaup" daddy picked up the line,
And that old mule started plodding along.

With feet hanging down from the rear,
We started out with much joy and cheer,
Dragging sticks in the dusty dirt,
making squiggles in the rut.
It was such a nice warm Spring day,
We were all so happy and gay,
We often burst into sporadic song.
And that old mule just plodded along.

Picking flowers along the road side,
Running to jump back in for a ride,.
The flowers looked pretty in the morning sun,
Too late Mama yelled "no not that one",
Stinging, the cactus to my hand clung.
Mama picked the burs out one by one,
I was soon back running and having fun,
As that old mule just kept plodding along.

At noon we stopped by a little stream,
Mama's fried chicken, biscuits tasted supreme.
While Mama and Daddy took a little snooze,
We kids pulled off our socks and shoes,
In the stream we went to splash and play,
Oh, what a wonderful, wonderful day!
Catching tadpoles with our hands,
Building castles in the wet sand,
While that old mule crunched on corn,

All too soon it was time to head home,
Exhausted, we were still glad we had come.
We had laughed and played, running free,
In the shade of that old spreading oak tree.
The ride home was longer and harder than before,
We were tired, wet, dirty, cranky, and slow,
Could not even muster up a song,
But that old mule just kept plodding along!

My mother was a woman of many talents. She would take scraps of cloth and create a beautiful quilt, or rocks and shells and make a lovely picture. She won ribbons at county fairs for many of her crafts. She always worked in her garden and canned many quarts of fruits and vegetables to feed her family throughout the winter months. She also wrote poetry and was published.

MY MOTHER

"Grandma Lively" as she was known to one and all,
Postman, banker, sons, cousins, not only the small.
She married "Jim Tack" when she was only fifteen,
Becoming mother to three children who were pre-teen.
Raised chickens, sold eggs, bought herself some land,
Ten children she bore, but she had only one husband.

She loved hoeing her garden and working in the sun,
Flowers, fruits and vegetables she grew for fun.
Cleaning, paring, steaming and canning in many a jar,
To feed thirteen children and visitors from near and far.
Always on Sunday after Church a crowd gathered to dine,
Enjoying fried chicken, biscuits and tasting syllabub wine.

She fashioned chambray, denim and twill into men's pants,
Working hard, selling to stores her nest egg to supplant.
She sewed the leftovers into school dresses for us girls,
Making them pretty with embroidered flowers and swirls.
To her grandchildren's delight she made them each a quilt,
Out of scraps, some appliqued with roses that don't wilt.

She drove a school bus full of children, nice or unruly,
Earning their love and respect and was called "Ms. Julia".
She had imagination, talents and ability plenty,
Her originality showed in gifts she made for many.
Ceramics, tin wreaths, pictures of cloth, rock or shell,
She won prizes at County Fair, gave gifts, but didn't sell.
A 1982 car was brought by this eighty-two year old dame,
Saying she hoped her children would be able to do the same.

Still later taking advantage of her age and health,
She loved getting attention and played it to the hilt
She enjoyed rocking and singing a lot of the time,
And lived to the ripe old age of Eighty-nine.

This tells it all—Mama was not a good housekeeper but she could grow a garden, can vegetables and put up vegetables for her family. She worked long hard hours in the garden and kitchen. Our pantry was always filled with good things to eat. I especially remember coming home from school to the smell of vegetable soup bubbling on the stove.

MAMA'S GARDEN

My mother was not good at keeping the home clean,
With ten children it was a job without end.

She would spend hours in the garden hoeing,
Get those vegetables up and growing.

Peeling, paring, preparing,
Getting ready for canning.

Pears, pickles, peaches,
On the stove steaming.

Tasting, stirring, seasoning,
ready in jars for sealing.

Our pantry was built from ceiling to floor,
4 x 4 with room to grow,
Always filled with good things to eat,
That Mama had from her garden made complete.

BLUE JEANS

Can you imagine a world without Blue Jeans?
Where shorts or skorts were never seen.
When ladies never wore mini skirts above the knees
And children didn't speak without saying Please.

Our noon meal is dinner—not lunch
We live in the country—don't get to town much.
Yet it is a happy and peaceful time,
Especially summer when school bells don't chime.

We love to read sitting under Joyce Kilmer's **"Trees"**
Enjoy the soft balmy summer breeze.
Dream of Edgar Allen Poe's beautiful **"Annabel Lee"**,
And wonder what it is like across the sea.

Disaster stole upon us out of the blue,
Our fun times became obscure.
The Japs struck with all their might,
Bombing Pearl Harbor at night.

Enlisting at once were all the farm men,
Our country they are ready to defend.
Women and children are put to the test,
Taking care of a farm and a crop to harvest.

Cotton to be picked, weighed and taken to the gin,
For help we had one old man and his women.
Mama gave us our brothers pants to wear,
Gathered at the waist to hold them there.

We left, giggling and singing, eager to start,
We'd show those guys who thought they were so smart.
Long before noon we are tired and lagging,
Down each row—our cotton sacks dragging.

Joyfully we watch our first hundred pounds weigh in,
Counting the money we now have to spend.
We can hardly wait to get to town as a team,
Anxious to buy a pair of "right" fitting Blue Jeans.

DESTINY

What could be more precious than four boys?
A sweet baby girl to bring love and joys.
Then one by one along came three girls more
That took away some of the joy and glow.

That baby grew to be a quiet little child
Who obeyed her parents and the rules they applied.
Kept to herself and spoke only when spoken to
She learned how to be Mama's helper for sure.

Growing up chubby freckled redheaded in her teens
Studying hard reading books and dreaming dreams
Of a knight in shining armor don't you see?
In real life a hard working carpenter was he.

A good wife homemaker and mother of five
Not so quiet now but happy and Oh so alive.

Morals truth and etiquette she did teach
With patience and love trying not to preach.

Now all five children are grown
With little ones all their own
Teaching them manners truth and morals strong
Though not the same as Mom's still not wrong.

Relishing the visits from them one and all
Cherishing the quiet time in between a call
Glad of a diversion or time for meditation
Still looking toward tomorrow with anticipation.

SILENT SALLY

Kids milling around here, there, and everywhere
among them a small child sitting on the bottom stair,
happy, listening to every word seemingly unaware,
Silent Sally is there—yes, she's THERE!!!

Silly teenage girls laughing without a care,
talking of boys, trying hard to be debonair,
giggling, snickering about secrets they share,
and Silent Sally is there, yes, she's THERE!!!

She listens with interest to her buccaneer
talk of his war experiences year after year,
sewing, reading or just rocking in her chair,
Silent Sally is there, yes, she's THERE!!!

The children all around dad, who has a flair
for the dramatic, always has a story to share
while she's in the kitchen among the earthenware,
but Silent Sally is there, yes she's THERE!!!

A dependable office worker, often called square
always on time, trustworthy, honest and sincere,
working hard amid slackers without despair,
Silent Sally is there, yes she's THERE!!!

When grandchildren come down the thoroughfare,
she's ready to soothe a hurt, dry many a tear,
lets the laundry go, as well as dirty tupperware,
Silent Sally is there, yes she's THERE!!!

They're growing older with gray and thinning hair,
she is reading or sewing but always will care,
for her buccaneer who can barely hear,
and Silent Sally is there, yes, she's THERE!!!

I graduated in 1944 during World War II. My graduating class hopefully anticipated the future as all graduates do. Since graduation we have had several reunions and keep in touch with class members. Our class was very small with only twenty-six to graduate.

THE CLASS OF FORTY-FOUR

It was the year of Nineteen Forty-four
In the midst of the Second World War
That the graduates of Waynesboro High,
Was determined to set the world on fire,
With their ambitions goals and plans.
Little did they know that destiny demands,
More give than take
More sow than make,
To achieve a satisfactory place,
In the whole of the human race.

Some achieved their goals,
Other re-aligned their roles,
While some lost their lives,
Making a dent in our archives,
Achieving fame,
Losing just the same.
But we are all tied together,
Because of our earlier tether,
Sitting side by side, day after day,
With teachers determined our minds to sway.

Today we are all separated by time and space,
But still some togetherness remains in place,
While we each go about our daily routines,
There are remembrances to be redeemed,
Stories to be told,
As memories unfold,
Giving us direction for guiding the young,
If to us they will hear listen and learn.
It is up to us to make them realize,
That life is more than dreams idealized.

-DICK

CHANGES

"What used to be is no more"

A lady stopped me the other day
And this is what she had to say.
"How do you get your hair so white?
Mine never turns out just right,
It's either too yellow or with a rinse blue,
Yours looks beautiful on you.
I'm sorry I didn't mean to be impolite,
But my hair always looks a fright".
I told her it was my natural hue,
To keep it clean I only use shampoo.
When I look in the mirror it's quite a shock.
Thinking my hair red, forgetting the clock,
Has constantly forged ahead,
Leaving behind an auburn redhead.

Another day my sister and I were in town,
When a lady motioned me to sit down.
As I approached she realized though,
That I was someone she didn't know.
When her friend walked in the super store,
My sister said that was who she mistook me for,
I replied but she has hair of white,
My sister informed me I needed to see the light.
That my hair was indeed very white.
To me it is red when out of sight.

People say you are as young as you feel,
Then a redhead I remain still,
Until a mirror shows a woman with white hair,
Looking back at me in total despair.

"What used to be is no more"

This is the story of how my husband and I met. Back in 1945 when he was on leave from the Army before being discharged. He had just gotten back to the United States from serving overseas during World War II.

GOLDEN MAGIC

September's golden leaves tumbling in the wind
glorious memories of earlier years begin to spin.

A soldier, a sailor and a girl came down the street
laughing and talking to the rhythm of their feet
as a lonely girl watched from her porch swing
while she listened for the telephone to ring.
The soldier started across looking her way
but the girl grabbed him saying, not today.
Several months later at the drug store they met
and the soldier told her of the day he lost his bet
To take the girl in the swing to the picture show
His sister grabbed his hand and wouldn't let go.

It was September just a year later that they wed
When the leaves were golden beginning to turn red.
Fifty golden years with September's chill in the air
She sits on the porch in her old rocking chair
When with his jaunty walk and winsome smile
He beckons her to come on outside.
He loves to watch the squirrels and birds feed
they throw them peanuts and sunflower seed.
As they stroll through the fallen leaves hand in hand
The magic's there in the golden years they've shared.

My husband always loved to fish and hunt. As a boy he was taught to follow the dogs and hunt by an uncle who lived near the woods.

THE HUNTER

He grew up loving the woods as a child
As he sloughed through swamps for many a mile,
Following an uncle and dogs hunting for coon
On bright nights lit by a big silvery moon.
In his teen years used his knowledge and hunting skill,
To keep the family's pantry and larder filled.

Back from the war and trying hard to forget
All the horrors and dangers he had met.
The "Old Man" was sick and in his last years,
Recalling his fox hunting days, his eyes in tears.
The woods with the pungent smell so close,
Offered peace to both in a big gulping dose.

He bundled the "Old Man" up and set out in the jeep,
To hear the dogs bay was enough to weep.
All across the woods, through swamps, up the hillside
They followed those hound dogs mile after mile
As they chased that fox scenting out his trail.
Outsmarted, the dogs came home dragging their tails.

Later when he needed to feed a family of seven
Dinner over, he often worked long after eleven.
His boat he kept on top his carpentry truck,
His way of relaxing was to try his luck.

At noon while taking a lunch break,
He could be seen out on a nearby lake.

Now he hunts deer with his sportsman knack,
Following their trail by checking their track,
His archery skills he has kept intact,
Using bow and arrow he's swift to strike,
Consciously taking only the meat he will need
His family and friends he will often feed.

He loves the woods, the forest and trees,
The wildlife, squirrels, rabbits, even the bees.
And in the hush of an early dewy morn,
Just as the sun begins to rise in the dawn,
Prayerfully he knows it was all created by God
Just as the Truth is revealed in His Word.

We always start the morning off with a prayer of thanksgiving at the breakfast table. At the noon hour our lunch is also blessed and also at the evening meal. When the children were small we put them to bed with a kiss and a prayer. This is one of my daughter, Lorene's favorite poems.

HE GIVES THANKS

As the morning sun rises in the east,
The birds start singing without cease.
The farmer rises early to start a new day,
With family breakfasting before going their way.,
He bows his head and gives THANKS!

With the sun high in the sky at noon,
He stops for a rest not a minute too soon,
The midday meal on the table waiting for him,
And though oft times its very, very slim,
He bows his head and gives THANKS !

With the sun setting in the east,
The chickens roosting on their nest,
Tired children all in their places,
With happy hearts and shiny faces,
He bows his head and gives THANKS!

As the moon shines down on the old homestead,
Kids all snug and cozy each in his own bed,
His wife ready to relate their latest caper,
Before settling down with the evening paper,
he bows his head and gives THANKS!

I wrote "Fifty Years" after a friend asked me to write a poem for her parents fiftieth anniversary. As my own marriage has lasted more than fifty years I could visualize the trials and the joys that had gone into fifty years of working together to raise a family, the happy as well as some sad times.

FIFTY YEARS

Fifty golden years we have shared
Letting the world know that we cared,
About each other and the commitment we made,
To always keep the promises that we gave.

Through the years there has been gladness,
Intermingled with some sorrows and sadness.
We are thankful for our Faith in God Above,
Who kept us together with His Love.

God gave us children for a little while,
And in our joy of them we smile.
He gave us the strength to keep them fed,
We thank the Lord for our daily bread.

The children are now grown and have left home,
With families and children of their own.
We by example have shown them truth and love,
Taught them to have Faith in God Above.

Our years together have been a blessing,
And as our days on earth are lessening,
We look forward to being Above the Bright Blue,
And spending Eternity with God and you.

In 1972 when my husband was fifty-two years old he was hospitalized three times within the year. The doctors did not diagnose his problem for several months. Then he was told he had a heart disease, put on tranquilizers and kept immobile for four years. At that time he was sent to the North Florida Regional Hospital for tests and open heart surgery. After having quadruple by-passes he recovered enough to get around some. Six years later he was again hospitalized and had another open heart surgery with triple by-passes that time. Then again in 1996 he went into the hospital with severe pains and had the third open heart surgery. After a year he needed more tests and another procedure and the doctors put a stint into one of his arteries.

ADJUSTMENT TO LIFE'S DIFFICULTIES

When just a young family man reaching his prime,
He was suddenly struck down without reason or rhyme.
Suffering severe heart pains and angina attacks,
Hurting, scared and not understanding the facts.
Doctors kept him immobile with prescribed "dope",
Using different medications to avoid a stroke.

For four long years, the time passed extremely slow,
Before even specialized doctors were in "the know",
Of arteriosclerosis, catheterization, and by-passing.
An operation to clear blocked arteries—What a Blessing!
Now he was able to hunt, fish and roam through the woods,
Much better but yet not well enough to work as he should.

So of necessity a house-husband he very reluctantly became,
Cleaning and cooking his freshly caught fish and game,
While his devoted wife, as a secretary, worked for pay.
He found it wasn't easy to stay home day after day.
Eventually he learned how to spend some quiet time.
Recording music, reading, even sewing to occupy his mind.
For twenty long years his pain and suffering we have shared,
The entire family grateful to God his life was spared.
Through the years he had so much to share: advice,
knowledge,
Something for all—even the ones who attend or teach college.
We have shared in his hobbies, often with tears and laughter,
Understanding one day there will be a pain-free Hereafter.

After suffering with heart problems for years my husband was having difficulty walking and the children got together and bought him a golf cart to get around the farm with. He has gotten much use out of it.

ZIPPING ALONG

Come ride with me in my yellow Club Car,
We won't go very fast or very far.
Just down to feed the chicken flock,
Through the horses and across the lot.
It makes the going easier by far,
Such a pleasure to ride in my Club Car.

Zipping in, zipping out, here, there, about,
My Club Car makes me gleefully shout!
In the rain it is the thing,
Makes getting the mail a fling!
Opening my electric gate,
Out we go at not so fast a rate.

Its parked just outside my door,
Ready at a moments notice to go.
To visit the neighbors where I couldn't walk before,
Or to look for a lost dog and much, much more.
THANKS, to my five wonderful kids,
Who do for me as I once for them did.

Several years ago one of our sons and his family were living in California. The oldest son graduated from High School and prepared to attend college. He chose Florida College and left home to come across Country. I wrote "A Fledgling's Flight" for his mother to ease her mind about her oldest child leaving home. Again when Chelsea Clinton the President's daughter decided to attend college across the Country from her home I revised "A Fledgling's Flight" to fit the occasion and sent it to the White House. I received a Thank You note.

A FLEDGLING'S FLIGHT

Today your oldest child began life as a freshman at college,
To gain self reliance, improve confidence and increase knowledge.
And even though he is some 3,000 miles away from his home,
You can rest assured that he is not afraid nor all alone.
For God walks beside him each day and holds his doubtful hand,
As he learns to cope with problems and live with his fellow man.
He had you for years to give him guidance and correction,
Now it is up to him to continue in the right direction.
As he holds tight to God's Word and studies hard each day,
For God will surely be there guiding him along the way.

LOVE IN BLOOM

She's seventeen and free as the wind
atop a Harley holding tight to her boyfriend.
All around his hometown they rode
Laughing, happy and very much in love.

He asked her to dinner at his parents home,
Excited and anxious she said she'd come.
Sunday dinner was always a treat
She was nervous his family to meet.

To this Yankee girl Sunday dinner meant sometime after three.
After late Saturday nights she slept the morning away, you
see.
Wanting so hard his folks to impress,
She went shopping for a brand new dress.

Southern tradition, Sunday dinner was always at noon
Preparations started early with the setting of the moon.
Church over, dinner ready and they **waited** and **w-a-i-t-e-d**,
Patience was wearing thin and soon dissipated.

The roar of that big motorcycle was finally heard,
The family got ready to greet this special girl.
So out to the porch with an anxious smile
They stood waiting their son and his girl to arrive.

Proud of her new dress, red nails gleaming in toeless shoes,
The girl beamed widely thinking she couldn't lose.
But then the dilemma hit her hard in the face,
How to alight gracefully, in a miniskirt, without showing her
lace.

The late hour, short miniskirt and painted toes,
This was the girl their son had chose.
But never an unkind word was said
She was welcomed and put at ease instead.

Soon this Rebel boy and Yankee girl were wed,
Traditions blended and a happy family was had.
Love, kindness, and encouragement is the key
Blending North and South into a strong family tree.

One of our grandsons left home to move across Country to go to college, dropped out after one year and bummed around for a year before meeting a nice girl who became his wife. She encouraged him to join the Army and he has excelled in his duties to his Country.

FULL CIRCLE

I'm moving out!
His thoughts almost a shout!
I'm tired of living under your thumb,
I'll make my own rules,—drop some!
Was the attitude of this seventeen year old
As he left for college feeling very bold.

One year of college was all he'd take,
For they, too, had restrictions and rules to make.
The next year he just bummed around,
earrings, tattoos, on his motorcycle all over town.
Shabby pants, dirty shirts, and worn out shoes
For this was the life style that he would choose.

At the club he met a nice young girl,
One whom he wanted to introduce to his Dad's world,
When he decided to make her his bride.
For her he knew he would need to provide,
The United States Army seemed the way,
Even with regulations he needed the pay.

He took to the Army like a duck to water,
Followed the commands the way he oughter.
In the Signal Corps school he did well,
Second in class he was one to excel.
Graduated with honors, beaming with pride
His beautiful wife smiling at his side.

Orders came to leave and head out west.
He made arrangements he thought was best,
To convoy with another was the plan, said he
They're flaky, freaky, earrings like we used to be.
But they are nice and will be a lot of support
As we travel to our new headquarters to report.

And so this young man as he turns twenty-one
Has come full circle with things he has learned.
He now has a good wife and a baby on the way
One that he is determined to care for each day
With his own rules and some regulations
His child will thrive from dad's delegations.

Ashton is the second son of my Dad's first wife. She died when he was a small boy. He and his older brother Louis were grown and married when I was born but I felt close to them and their families as I spent a lot of time visiting them, probably because I made a good baby sitter.

ASHTON

When I was still very small,
Ashton had a wife and two kids, I recall.
He was already grown, and a family man,
One who loved to tinker on cars first hand.
Joan was born later after they moved away,
So when they visited it was a happy day.

Once they took me and the kids to a dance,
It was fun to watch the grownups prance.
I sat and fed a bottle to Annie Lee,
With Julian sitting entranced at my knee.
We enjoyed listening to the band,
All too soon was overcome by the sandman.

Once He got his jalopy running smooth and true.
And took me for the fastest ride I ever knew.
Shaking in my seat, with my heart plinking,
It ran like he had never done any tinkering.
Much later I exclaimed ever so proud,
"We went over a hundred miles an hour"!

Ashton and Stella's life was sort of up and down,
But through it all a family man he was found.
And with them I always felt secure.
He was my Big brother I knew for sure.
I'll never forget his last 4th of July,
When we all knew it was our last good bye.

I'm reminded of that beautiful song we always sing
"Till we meet again", as my eyes with tears sting.
Its true togetherness we all share,
As time passes and we show that we care.
With joy in our family and the simple things,
Always the harmony that being together brings.

Stella's last testimony certainly was not idle,
To Ashton family was important and vital,
though he had for a birth mother, another
He respected and always called Mama, Mother.
To me he will always be my Big brother,
Just like him, there'll never be another.

Evelyn ("Ebba")was my sister born to my dad's first wife. She died giving Ebba birth. Ebba was raised by an aunt and when dad married my mother Ebba had become a part of their household and continued to live with them most of the time. I went to college, then came home during the war. No cars were available so I lived in town with Ebba and her family and walked back and forth to work. Ebba's oldest daughter says she feels like we are sisters more than aunt and niece.

"EBBA"

"Ebba" was my inspiration during her life.
My sister taught me by example to be a good wife.
All about being a family and having a close bond,
One that would withstand the world and its harm.

Once when I was about six years old,
She was my "half" sister I was told.
Proud of having something different and new,
(Remember this was from a child's point of view.)
I was singing and skipping with a lilting pace,
When she grabbed my arm and shook her finger in my face
"If you can't claim whole kin don't claim any at all!"
I knew then that family was A-One even tho I was small.

Fresh out of college I took a job down the street,
Walked to and from work each day of the week.
For some baby-sitting I received room and board,
While lessons from her were intuitively sowed.
By example Ebba taught me to be a good mother,
To be conscientious & respect the property of another,
To leave another's mail and personal items alone,
She became my mentor, one for me to admire and clone.

I learned a lot about how to deal with a bunch of kids,
From changing diapers, playing dolls to teenage fads.
I learned how to bake a delicious caramel cake,
To wash dishes and wrinkle free beds to make.
Her house was always clean and dust free,

How she did it was amazing to me!
I believed she loved to read a good book,
Almost as much as she loved to cook.

I've quoted her sayings many a time,
When certain things pop into my mind.
Through the years from her I took my cue,
Dearly loved,—honor and respect was her due.

When Mama's oldest child was born he wasn't given a name for almost two years. The reason being, Daddy didn't want to name a child a common name. Daddy went to a funeral once where all the pallbearers including himself were named Jim The person who had died was also named Jim. So daddy decided to give his children names no one else would have. He picked the initials Q.U. for the first child and it was later that they found the name Quartus Urbane in the book of Romans to go with the initials. He always wore a hat declaring that it was Q.U.'s hat, so I wrote a poem for his birthday using that as a theme. Q.U., like his Daddy before him, used walks to teach his children and grandchildren about nature.

Q. U. EIGHTY YEARS

HAPPY BIRTHDAY TO YOU, Q.U.!
I''VE NO "HAT"—WILL A POEM DO?

We are glad you are going strong at eighty,
Taking long walks almost daily,
To your grand children's delight,
Who get to tag along when the sun is bright.

You teach them about trees, tracks, plants and such,
That's an education not found in books.
We wish for you many more joys,
With all these wonderful girls and boys.

Q.U. totes a hoe when he goes for his hikes,
To dig the wild flowers that he sights.
He plants them in his back yard,
Has the prettiest plants in the neighborhood.

HAPPY BIRTHDAY TO YOU, Q. U.!
This is my prayer for you,
That you have many more,
And enjoy them as never before.

(P.S. Q.U. passed away at age 83 and his hoe was decorated by his grandchildren with flowers he had grown. His hoe stood along with all the other flowers at his funeral.)

My brother Van grows sugar cane rising early in the morning to plow the fields and staying late in the evening to get it ready for grinding and making cane syrup.

THE SUGARCANE MAN

Daily from sun up to sun down
He plows and plants the ground,
Grows the best Sugar Cane around
He's called the Sugarcane man
His real name is Van.
He waters and hoes day after day,
Until that cane is ready with its hay
To be stripped and hauled to the mill,
Squeezed its juice flows from the still.
Sweet to the taste, a mouth watering thrill.
Into an old iron pot for cooking it goes,
Stirring and skimming with long handled gourds,
The syrupy smell tickles his nose,
when its bottled for sale at last,
And the Sugarcane man has finished his task.

People come from all directions,
To taste and buy this rare confection,
Their sweet tooth makes the connection,
With the Sugarcane man who greets with a smile,
Those whose tastes brings them many a mile.

Van also enjoys working in his fields of cane, peas and corn; when he does he wears the shabbiest clothes he has. The first time a nephew (who had just married into the family) saw him he was aghast at his clothing and wanted to go into town immediately and buy him some better clothing. Later he saw him dressed for Church and realized his mistake.

UNCLE SOCKS

Once there was a man who always dressed down
He wore clothes made for the rag man or clown
While he worked in his garden and cane fields,
He Was never one to worry about appearances.
One day when he stopped to take a rest,
He pulled off his shoes, his socks were a mess,
Toes covered with mud cause his socks had holes,
This didn't bother him as his shoes had soles.
Aghast was the newest member of his family,
Who couldn't understand why we let him be,
To wear his rags and wanted to buy him socks,
To keep his feet clean and warm when feeding stock.
Then one day he ran into him in the town,
Now he neither looked ragged or like a clown,
But was spanking clean and neatly dressed,
For he was wearing his Sunday best.
So from that day to this,
He was known for his un-dress,
And was called "Uncle Socks"
Lovingly and without any "Knocks"

Another brother was a big deer hunter and could tell the most interesting hunting tales. I did go hunting with him and my husband one morning. The result was I sat, cold and freezing and decided never to go again.

A ONE NIGHT HUNTING STAND

Uncle Keely's hunting tales were such a ploy,
To hear,
to remember,
to enjoy!

So one day I thought I'd try my hand,
And I let him put me in a tree stand.
Where I sat,
still-
without a sigh

Hoping that 'ole deer would just stroll by,
Then I would shoot him
BANG-
right in the eye!

Uncle Keely says deer are so cunning,
They know when men for them are gunning,
They will cross the road-
backing back,
To keep men and dogs off their track.

So as I sat cold,
freezing in my seat,
That sly deer circled and he lay fast asleep,
Almost at my dangling feet

laughing! Don't you see
At ME,
Foolish 'ole ME!

Yes, Uncle Keely's hunting tales were such a ploy,
To hear,
To remember
To enjoy!

Our brother Louis was the oldest of my dad's children. His mother died when he was just a small boy and he was only 2 years younger than my mother. He always called her "Mama" and had a lot of love and respect for her. Louis was almost forty years old when the youngest child was born. Daddy liked to claim that he had children "from no teeth to no teeth". Louis often visited unexpected and it was always a joy to see him.

UNEXPECTED VISITS

When I was a child, very small
a tall slender man would come to call.
We never knew when he would stop by,
He tried hard to keep the family tie.

We always hated to see Louis go,
Not knowing when he would knock on the door.
His unexpected visits brought many joys,
To the family, especially the little girls and boys.

We thought a city fellow we'd charm,
And showed him all around the farm.
Hazel and Jean sometimes came too,
Our hearts rejoiced greeting them anew.

I grew up, married and had a child.
Into my hospital room Louis came with a smile.
Thirteen months later we had another boy.
Again in walked Louis, much to my joy.

His unexpected visits were always a pleasure.
His quiet demeanor and smile truly a treasure.
He was always there when you least expect,
I remember him for visits with great respect.

My sister Atta Lee was the dare devil of five sisters, always daring one or all of us to take a risk. She was always the one to climb the highest tree, walk through briers or muddy branches. My family moved to Florida in 1954, she with her husband and daughter moved a year or two later. Atta lost her husband at a young age and she and her daughter became an important part of our family. Always enjoying family dinners, birthdays, holidays and special occasions with us. My kids always looked forward to seeing their Aunt Atta especially when she came with her wonderful pound cake or a pot of field peas.

MY SISTER

As a child she had straight boyish cut hair,
In a minute would take on most any dare.
She was our own tomboy for sure,
Who loved to tease and always to out-do.
She would climb to the highest tree top,
Always making me look like a flop.
She loved the outdoors and to fish the lake,
Hoeing the garden and having leaves to rake.
She always seem to come out ahead,
No matter what anyone did or said.

Now a mother and grandmother of two,
She has shown she can surely endure,
Under stress having lost her husband,
Working hard she kept her family in hand.

She loves her garden and working in the yard,
Sewing, quilting, for her nothing seems hard.
Her canning and freezing—none can compare.
As a Christian she loves to give and share.
She's my sister and on her I depend,
To be there as a very special friend.

Knowing God, Loving God and being a child of God, with a strong faith in God is the foundation on which this assurance is built. It all comes together in a circle, God, family and earth.

My family and I had fixed up a basket of place mats, candles, candle holders, dish towels, a framed poem as well as one of my poetry books for a nephew's wedding/shower gift. At the shower another niece re-marked what a nice heritage to have and keep. That remark and a book I was reading about the life cycle of wolves brought into being this poem.

CIRCLE OF LIFE

God used His Power to create in circles,
The sun, moon and the stars that glow,
The earth and all living things that grow.
He breathed life into man, from dust we come,
and to dust we must go.

It is often said that love makes the world go round,
The axle upon which it turns is Gods Love,
family traditions, and the tie that binds.
For God so loved the world that He gave
His only Begotten Son for redemption of mankind.

As you travel along the circle of life in your time,
keep the faith, the love of God and remind
your children the importance of family ties.
Give them a heritage of which to be proud,
and leave an enduring legacy behind.

SUNSHINE OF GOD'S LOVE INSPIRATIONAL POEMS

A lot of my poems are inspired by sermons or Wednesday night talks that I have heard. I have jotted down ideas and come home and put them in the form of a poem. I also got a lot of my inspiration for poems from nature. Taking walks in the park, or through the deep woods, or just in my back yard listening to the birds singing sweetly in the trees. "A Beautiful Story" was inspired by a young preacher telling the story found in Nehemiah and the rebuilding of the temple and how the people worked together. I used this poem as a background for bringing two factions together in unity at the office where I worked.

A BEAUTIFUL STORY

In the Bible a beautiful story is told
Of Nehemiah and the people of old.
When the rebuilding of walls of Judah was begun
They started by praying to God in Chapter One.
With all people of every tribe and nation,
Helping each other with the restoration.
Men, women, and children side by side did toil,
As block after block was laid in the wall.
The wall finished to the top they climbed,
With thankful hearts and hands entwined,
Joyful songs echoed throughout the night,
As each sang with all their spiritual might.
People today a new life can also build,
By studying God's Word and doing His Will.
So Christians with spiritual voices blend,
As they join each other in the fight against sin.

"A Circle Of Faith" was written after Colin Williamson preached a sermon using a chart to demonstrate. He used my poem later to finish up the sermon.

A CIRCLE OF FAITH

As a **whole Body** of God's people who care,
The Truth of God's Word we share.
We want to always with our **touch**,
Share the warmth of our Church.

To tell our **friends** every day
That God sent His Beloved Son to show us the Way,
To give them the message of Truth and Love
That came down from Heaven Above.

That all can be baptized with Spiritual Grace,
Living daily to meet Him face to face.
We want to assimilate His Holy Word,
Get involved as we should.
Study, work and grow.
To others God's Love show,

**Becoming a whole Body doing His Will
And the circle of Faith will be fulfilled.**

ALMOST

Pilate almost let Jesus go
his heart filled with sorrow and woe.
He gave into the pressure at hand
listened to prevailing voices of man.

Pilate asked Jesus, are you the Jews' King,
Do you on this earth want to reign?
My Kingdom is not of this world", said He.
I deliver the Truth to make men free".

Though Pilate could find no fault in Him,
he would not go out on a limb,
to save Jesus from an angry mob.
They cried, free the man who would rob.

Thrice Pilate asked what evil has this man done,
saying I find no fault in him as his hands he wrung.
The Jews were insistent that Jesus be crucified
With loud voices they shouted and cried.

Pilate almost let Jesus go
his heart filled with sorrow and woe.
Not wanting to be found at fault
Pilate washed his hands for naught.

BELIEVE (in) GOD

I believe God reigns in Heaven Above
I believe in His Wonderful Love.
I believe He gave His only begotten son
I believe the Bible is His Holy Word.

I believe in God—but do I believe God?
Do I believe His Word?
Do I believe what He doth say?
Do I believe enough to obey?

You believe in God who lives on High
You believe He made the earth and sky.
You believe He gave birds wings to fly.
You believe He sent Jesus to die.

You believe in God—but do you believe God?
Do you believe His Word?
Do you believe what He doth say?
Do you believe enough to obey?

We believe in God's Saving Grace
We believe He loves the whole human race
We believe He forgives us our sin
We believe He will save all repenting men.

We believe in God—but do we believe God?
Do we believe His Word?
Do we believe what He doth say?
Do we believe enough to obey?

"Christian Women" was written for the second meeting of our Ocala Ladies weekend sessions, using the theme that was selected as the topic of our discussions. Studying these women of the Bible gives us inspiration of how women today can put God's Word to use in our every day life.

CHRISTIAN WOMEN

Make us as Clay in the Potter's Hand
Mold us into beautiful women of His land

Meditating on these Biblical women can be fulfilling.
Look for traits worthy of our consideration in living.
In the Scriptures we read of the women of old
Of their courageous lives we are told.
These examples were given to us beforehand
Our own qualities to search for and understand.

It took courage for Sarah at the God's command,
To follow Abraham to a strange land.
Ruth gave up her home and family for something better,
Faith in the God of her dead husband's mother.
Beautiful brave Esther when she was made queen of the land,
Fulfilled God's will by saving her people with a clever plan.
Elizabeth in prayer reached out to her cousin with love,
Mary, who was blessed with child from God Above.
Martha, a good hostess was busy with household tasks,
Mary sat, listened and had questions of the Lord to ask..
Dorcas full of good works and charitable deeds,
Sewed and made coats for widows who had needs.
When Lydia was baptized she rejoiced and appealed

Paul to come to her house for lodging and a meal.
Mary worried when Jesus in the temple was lost,
Stood patiently by and watched His death on the Cross.

We each with our own personalities set to the work of the
Lord,
Can blend and create a bonding worthy of love.
Our indomitable spirits and reassuring smiles
Will help carry our troubles through many miles.
Our patience, love of God's Word and all that's true,
Will make us trustworthy, loyal, Christians that are pure.

Make us as clay in the Potter's hand
Mold us into beautiful women of His land

CELEBRATIONS OF THE HEART

**Ecstasy comes with truth knowing
Warming the heart to glowing!**

Joy in the heart starts the very first day,
The Word is heard and a decision made to obey.
As a babe in spirit earnestly longing for the Word,
In Worship the Lord's Supper is observed.
Steadfastness and truth become a way of life,
Keeping away all greed, envy and strife.

God fills the heart with heavenly love, Trust
Confidence, Faith and humility a must.
The joy of salvation will soar as an eagle,
Forgiveness of sins is uplifting and regal.
The heart in instruction will rejoice,
Words of wisdom are heard by choice.

On the day of redemption a jubilee is heard,
Saints praising God for revealing His Word.

Those who are faithful to the end,
ever God's Word willing to defend,
Will have their names written in gold,
Together with the Saints of old.

Ecstasy comes with truth knowing
Warming the heart to glowing!

Scott Conley preached about Consequences in a sermon and I was impressed with his thoughts enough to try to capture it in poetry form. Sermons I have heard as well as Bible studies and just living a Christian life are reflections of my poems. Several of my inspirational poems have been published in church bulletins all across this Country from Florida, Georgia, Texas and California.

CONSEQUENCES

Jesus, in the garden prayed "Thy Will be done"
Waking the disciples he said "the hour has come
Judas for thirty pieces of silver parlayed
Then with a kiss the son of God betrayed.

Three times impetuous Peter the Lord Denied
When he recalled the words of Jesus he cried.
The mob freed Barabbas and had Christ crucified
The Son of God suffered on the cross and died.

Stephen by signs and wonders made the Word known,
Accused of blasphemy he was taken out and stoned.
Ananias and Sapphira for profit lied
They tested the Holy Spirit and they died.

Saul persecuted all the Christians he could find
On the Damacus road the Lord struck him blind.
Paul was told what he must do to be saved
He received his sight when he obeyed.

IN LOVE AND TRUTH WE ARE FORGIVEN
WITH GOD'S GRACE WE CAN SEE HEAVEN.

Our Poetry club was given Anxiety as the subject to write a poem for our following meeting. In thinking about anxiety I could not help thinking of the assurance that God gives each of us through His Word. "Darkness and Light" was also published in our local Church bulletin.

DARKNESS AND LIGHT

anxiety
silently as a little mouse it creeps
along dark halls with shadows so deep
Sneaking, stalking it's prey,
Making worry lines along the way.
Fear creeping up my spine,
Leaving behind,

ANXIETY !!!!!

ASSURANCE
LOVE GLOWING LIKE A CANDLE FLAME,
WARMING HEARTS, ONE AND ALL THE SAME
GUIDING, LEADING TOWARD A BETTER WAY!
WITH ROD AND STAFF HELPING THE STRAY
ONWARD, UPWARD, TO A BRIGHTER DAY
THAT'S GOD'S WAY !
ASSURANCE !!!!!!!!!!

I've been asked to write poems for several of our Vacation Bible Schools. I wrote "Emotions" to help the children learn about different feelings and emotions.

EMOTIONS
(Feelings)

EXPECTATION (Hope)
In Vacation Bible School studying is fun,
Of Jesus' last Days on earth we learn

EXASPERATION (Irritation)
Alone in the Garden Jesus prayed and wept, As his beloved
disciples slept.

DESPERATION (Despair)
Last Supper Jesus gave Thanks and broke bread
Woes to the one who will betray the Head.

ISOLATION (Loneliness)
On the Cross our sins Jesus bore
In agony He suffered there alone.

RESURRECTION (Rebirth)
Fulfilling the scriptures he rose again
In Heaven with God He will reign.

EXULTATION (Joy)
When we attend Vacation Bible School
We learn to follow the Golden Rule.

EVERLASTING JOY

Joy comes softly in the morning
As day begins its dawning.
God loves and is always nigh
He lives and reigns on High.
Joy comes with knowledge of God
As we live daily by His Word.
With faithfulness our sins we cease,
We gain patience, kindness and peace
.The joy we find in the Glory of God,
Is filled with happiness and love,
An inner peace that holds us secure,
For God's Word forever is true.
Joy found within one's own heart,
Is everlasting and solid as a rock.
It's something no other can take away.
Sharing Joy multiples it more each day.

ENCOURAGEMENT

Encouragement comes in many forms from various places,
With love and kindness from numerous different races.
A handshake, a friendly smile or a pat on the shoulder,
Giving love, warmth, hope and friendship to the beholder.

Hearing a small child praying to God,
The elderly seem to be everywhere on this sod.
Please take care of these old people,
Some are sick and others very feeble.

Or to see a young man cutting the grass,
For one who had lost her companion of years past.
A grieving widow now all alone,
Still offering hospitality in her home.

Also to see other young people being a friend,
To the older folks who now have to depend,
On others to ease their aches and pain,
Knowing that to die in Christ is but gain.

Young men who take a leadership role,
Preaching and teaching to some lost soul.
Leading the congregation in singing praise,
And to God their voices in prayer, raise.

Young women taking flowers or an unexpected present,
To a shut-in or a local nursing home resident.
Teaching youngsters in the Bible classes,
All about how Jesus was feeding the masses.

Older people teaching the very young,
By example in God's Word to be strong.
Everyone working in God's Kingdom together,
Bonding in communication with love for each other.

GOD'S AMAZING GRACE

It's Amazing that Almighty God gave His Only Son,
And more amazing that over death Victory was won.
By God's loving Mercy we get not what we deserve,
If we give mercy to others—then God we serve.

God's Amazing Grace is shown in many earthly places,
His wonderful gifts are given to all the human races.
The sun, moon, stars that shine 'oer all the land,
The rain that causes flowers to bloom ever so grand.

Amazing also is the Work that Christ Jesus has done,
When He died on the cross for each and everyone.
Those willing to accept His wonderful gift of Love,
Obeying God, doing His Will are assured of a home above.

We get that which we do not have coming to us,
But because of God's Mercy when we return to dust,
We can live with Jesus in a Heavenly Home in the sky.
"Thank You God for sending Jesus" is our humble cry!

The Ocala Ladies Weekend meeting for the third time featured Fruit of the Spirit and I was again asked to write a poem to illustrate the meaning of Fruit of The Spirit from a woman's viewpoint. Later I found out they were using gardening as the theme and wrote a second poem also.

FRUIT OF THE SPIRIT

A woman kneads her family together
Blending them with love forever.
She is very conscious of a healthy diet,
To ensure her family's meals are just right.
That their home life is filled with fruit of the Spirit,
And the devil and his helpers will not inherit.

Joyously she evenly fills each bowl,
With God's Word stirring every soul.
Mixing all with Serenity and Peace,
To break asunder the devil's lease.
Trusting the Truth that she heard,
She carefully instructs them in God's Word,

Her long Suffering, gentleness and a kind heart
Blended with faith and goodness gives them a firm start.
Mixed altogether with patience and self-control,
Lets them know that they can be on God's Heavenly Roll.
As we follow her daily diet with care,
We too, God's Holy Word can Share.

Galations 5:22-23, NKJV—"But the fruit of the Spirit is
love, joy, peace, longsuffering, kindness, goodness,
faithfulness, gentleness, self-
control. . . . "

GOD CARES FOR US

The birds as they fly through the air
have no thought of raiment or worldly care,
neither the field lilies who are arrayed in Glory
but we through His Word learn the Gospel Story.

God in His Mercy cares for us if we believe, obey and trust.

Just as the flowers, one by one, bloom
God will take care of our doubt and gloom,
when with Faith our confession we give
and promise a Christian life to live.

God in His Mercy cares for us if we believe, obey and trust.

As sure as bees honey doth make
when into our lives Christ we take,
we let our anxiety for tomorrow go
and to others His Love show.

God in His Mercy cares for us if we believe, obey and trust.

GOD'S PLAN

Before the beginning of time God had a Plan
the manifestation of which was to save man,
who being made in God's very own image,
upon birth would embark on life's pilgrimage.

A journey to take him through this life
with many a snare, troubles and strife.
It will be man's own decision to make
and to determine which path he will take.

The journey with worldly charms and pleasure,
or one of Godly Love and Heavenly treasure.
The devil is out to entrap everyone he can,
And only with God's Grace does man win.

We can all share in the Heavenly Home Above
that God has prepared with unsurpassed Love.
Love so great that He gave His Only Son,
that we, free from sin, may become One.

With Jesus our Redeemer, we have Salvation,
Which God gives to each and every generation.

GOD'S POWER

The Glory of morning when dawn starts
When the sun rising in the East sparks
A continuous warmth to last all day
Giving us hope with each shining ray.

The glimmer of a bright moon at night
Guides us with God's Eternal Light
As it flows 'oer all earth and oceans deep
Proving security and peace as we sleep.

The twinkling of thousands of stars above
Reminds us constantly of God's Enduring Love
And the vast greatness of Jesus' Sacrifice
Securing our hearts by His Mercy and Grace.

Each second and minute of every day and hour
Seeing the evidence of God's Great Power
In all things that grow so beautiful and tall
In thunder, lightening and raindrops as they fall.

We hear His Voice in the rustling wind
And on Him we must surely learn to depend
For all our daily strength and might
Living in His Holy Word day and night.

GOD'S SAVING GRACE

In Jesus we find Peace and Love,
One sent with God's Grace from Above.
From the clutches of sin, God saves man,
And gives him hope of living in Gloryland.

When man was deep in sin and its slave,
Christ came into this world all men to save.
Through God's Word we need to hear and obey,
With pain and anguish our debt Jesus did pay.

By God's Grace our sins he bore,
A crown of thorns on His brow He wore.
Now through His blood we have hope,
As Faith comes to us by what the Apostles wrote.

From all our sins we need to repent,
Because we know from God, Jesus was sent.
We must confess His name before men,
Acknowledging our love and sin.

By Faith we go down into waters of Baptism,
Knowing that we'll live with the Christ risen,
If a faithful life we continue to live,
By God's Grace and His love to others give.

GOD'S WORLD

The early morning dewy mists,
Sun peeping through snowy cirrus,

Birds singing sweetly in the trees,
Nectar seeking bumble bees.

The flutter of pretty butterfly wings,
Above the bounty of verdant growing things.

Glorious flowers with fragrant bloom,
A huge spherical glowing moon.

Displays God's Power and Might,
Safely secures us in the night.

I wrote "I've Got Faith" when a friend was in the hospital. The original title was: Hallelujah! I've got faith. When my friend Myrtle Silas was diagnosed with cancer and facing death. She showed such great courage and faith in dealing with her illness it inspired me to change the title. "I've Got Faith" was read at her funeral services.

I'VE GOT FAITH

Tho' this old body is racked with sores and pain,
I won't let sorrow and despair over me reign.
Hallelujah! I've Got Faith

Faith that Jesus for me is always near,
Giving me comfort through friends so dear.
This body is only made of bone and mucilage
But my soul is made in God's very own Image.
Hallelujah! I've Got Faith

Faith that Jesus Christ is God's Own Son
And that victory over death He won.
As my last days on this earth come to an end,
The Gospel of Christ to death I'll defend.
Hallelujah! I've Got Faith

That God in Heaven is waiting there for me,
And at last from sin and pain I'll be free.
Hallelujah! I've Got Faith!

JOY IN THE MORNING

Start your day with a cheery good morning smile,
  Grin a little—maybe laugh once in a while!
Show kindness, compliments and grace without guile,
  People will soon become accustomed to your style!

Ditch your worries and disgust in the trash,
  Discard them as easily as residue and ash.
Take your troubles to the Lord in Prayer,
  Bundle them all up and leave them there.

Don't hide your feelings under the cover,
  You need to be either one way or the other.
There is no room in your heart for sadness,
  When it is full of joy, love and gladness!

Riding along a Georgia country road one lonely night I watched the darkness slip by, unable to tell if I was looking out at forest or farm land, I felt the darkness closing in. Then I noticed house lights off in the distance and realized I was not alone. I felt much safer knowing people lived near by and felt they would be willing to help if we had car trouble. I wondered if this was the way fishermen feel when they see the beacon of the lighthouse. "Lights of Comfort" has been used for get well cards to comfort sick friends, and my youngest son used it as an eulogy for one of his friends at the Sheriff's Department.

LIGHTS OF COMFORT

God is the Creator of all darkness and light,
Even the tiniest beam shows His Power and Might.
The tiny fireflies light glows brightly in the dark,
As they flutter to and fro across the
evergreen park.

A single candle burning on the sill of
the window,
Sheds its light making shadows seem
as a rainbow.
House lights scattered here and there
along country nooks,
Lets you know its not as lonely and
desolate as it looks.

A beacon turning round and round
brightly lights the sky,
Guiding planes to earth and com-
forts pilots as they fly.

Harbor lights illuminate the cutters path to shore,
Giving fishermen encouragement to toss the net once more.

The greatest light of all time and dimension,
Is God's Love when He in His Grace and Wisdom,
Sent His Son, Jesus as the Light of the World,
To give all mankind a gift of life eternal.

"Master Gardners" was the second poem written for our third Ocala Ladies Weekend. I wrote two poems, I didn't know which fit the scheme of things better but we decided to use both. One for Friday evening and one again on Saturday.

MASTER GARDENERS

Christian Women master gardeners can be,
Sowing Fruit of the Spirit for all to see!

Planting God's Word in fertile soil,
Watering it daily with Spiritual oil.
Tending it carefully with Joy and Love,
That we receive from God Above.
Fertilizing with Goodness growth begins,
And continues with repenting of sins.
With Patience cultivating the Truth we heard,
Weeding out sin with gentleness and a kind word.
With faithfulness hoeing broken ground,
Spreading The Gospel and Peace all around.
Using Self-Control as a rake,
Rambling words we dissipate.
As we watch our gardens grow,
We harvest fruit from seeds we sow.

Christian Women master gardeners can be,
Sowing Fruit of the Spirit for all to see.

"Obedience" was written for Vacation Bible School using the theme that was selected for the children that year.

OBEDIENCE

WHAT HAPPENED WHEN JONAH RAN AWAY
AND GOD HE DID NOT OBEY?
COME TO VACATION BIBLE SCHOOL AND LEARN
WHAT HAPPENED AT THE SEA.

COME HEAR, COME SEE
WHAT WE DO AT VBS - YES!

WHY DID GOD BLESS ABRAHAM
WHEN HE DID NOT FALTER?
COME TO VACATION BIBLE SCHOOL AND LEARN
WHAT HAPPENED AT THE ALTAR.

COME HEAR, COME SEE
WHAT WE DO AT VBS - YES!

WHY WAS NAAMAN PICKED BY GOD
TO SHOW HIS LOVE AND POWER?
COME TO VACATION BIBLE SCHOOL AND LEARN
WHAT HAPPENED IN THE CLEANSING HOUR.

COME HEAR, COME SEE
WHAT WE DO AT VBS - YES!

WHERE DID GOD TELL JOSHUA TO GO
PROMISED NEVER TO FORSAKE HIM IF HE

WOULD DO SO?
COME TO VACATION BIBLE SCHOOL AND LEARN
WHAT JOSHUA DID IN JERICHO.

COME HEAR, COME SEE
WHAT DO WE DO AT VBS - YES!

"Our Minister" is for and about our dearly beloved minister, Colin Williamson, who has worked with this congregation for over thirty years and has been a great comfort to this family especially in times of sickness. We love and thank him.

OUR MINISTER

Our minister is a man of boundless energy,
One who always has a story to share,
He has been with us for thirty years,
A righteous, God-fearing man of integrity.
In the pulpit he's a master
Never forgetting the point he is after,
And he sticks even if its past time
For another soul is always his goal.

You can find him in hospital corridors,
Supporting family and friends for hours,
While waiting for a doctor's report, beside a bed,
In a waiting room or even a hall he bows his head.
Inside a Courtroom or a Judge's Chamber
Assisting a family and a troubled teenager,
He's there and you know he will always care,
With an arm around a shoulder or a knee bent in prayer.
At the grave side of a cherished brother,
He consoles—but not like any other.
He had held his hand to the very end,
Shared moments with Jesus, their friend.
His family often catches him going out the door,
An errand to run, a friend to see, much more.

He stops to hear their words and thoughts,
And give thanks for all the joys God has brought.

A ball game is his forte',
A chance to extol makes his day.
He stays to the bitter end—lose or win,
It doesn't matter—he's O.K.
He is a man of courage and honor,
A friend to one and all. He will be with each of us to the end,
His good will and spirit won't bend.
He is there whenever we need him, Just a call away
-any time night or day.

A simple "Thank You" is not enough.
For all the prayers, deeds and sacrifice he has made for us.
We are Happy today because
HE WALKS WITH US,
HE TALKS WITH US,
STAYS WITH US,
AND HE PRAYS WITH US.

I am a member of the International Society of Poets and this is my part of a poem for world wide peace that each member was asked to write.

PEACE

The Peace that He gives to us
Is filled with Love and Trust.
As the glowing sun rises in the East
it fills my heart with Joy and Peace.

A daily walk takes me out past a sleepy town as it begins to
awake,
Down through the meadow to a mist covered little lake.
A Mother goose and her goslings enjoy an early morning swim.
The birds are singing royal from the highest tree limb.
Morning doves cooing to each other, as they feed from the
ground.
Frisky squirrels chasing another, happy as they run around.
Retracing my steps morning smells tickle my nose,
Joy and Peace within swells and restores my soul.

Looking back over the years of toil and sweat,
that it took to raise a family with no regret.
As the sun begins to sink slowly in the West
I'll lay my head down to a peaceful rest.

"Peace I leave with you. My Peace I give to you" John 14:27 NKJV

PROMISES AND BLESSINGS

God is Faithful His promises to keep,
He is ever watchful for straying sheep.
Our prayers He has promised to hear,
When we petition through Christ His Heir.
He has promised us life with Him above,
Secured with trust and Heavenly Love.

Many blessings God has bestowed upon us,
Among which is the ability to love and trust.
We portray God's love and power,
As we live for Christ, hour by hour.
God gives us a spirit of gentle and quiet beauty,
As we diligently perform our Christian duty.

We receive blessings through friendship,
With other Christians in a caring kinship.
Our service to others is a blessing true,
Showing God's love when for others we do.
Conducting our life daily in a spiritual walk,
Brings us closer to God without fault.

We have happiness and joy in God Above,
When we continue to communicate His Great Love.
We trust that for us in the end it will be said,

That we have done what we could the Gospel to spread.
Having finished our work on this earth and we die,
We are promised a home with Jesus on High.

Faith in God has provided me with inspiration for many poems. Sermons I have heard as well as Bible classes and just living the Christian life are reflections of my poems. "Reflection" was written for our first Ocala Ladies Weekend. I struggled with this one as I didn't know exactly what the ladies in charge of the program were planning. They have encouraged me to write for other meetings for several years now. After much thought and reflection knowing it was for a group of Christian women, I was able to write the following. I included in it names of women using characteristics found in the Bible.

REFLECTION

As the glorious sun was setting in the west,
Heavenly glows upon the earth were cast.
A woman, her family settled and evening chores done
Strolled slowly along the river bank to be alone.
She stood on the bridge looking into the river
As the rushing water tumbled and swirled silver.
Her thoughts as in a dream became enshrined
Reflected were the souls of all mankind.

*Deep in the dark murky waters caught in the
Dangerous undertow,
Were idolaters, the liars, the greedy, masters of
Deception,
The selfish, those of little faith, the ones who had
Sunk so low.
Floating above the dark waters were God's saved
Children,
Full of compassion, forgiveness, courage, the faithful*

Few,
Those of human kindness, with generous loving hearts
The ones without sin.

She stood with thanksgiving in her heart and looked
To the heavens above,
She saw Hope, Faith, Mercy and Grace securely enfolded
In the arms of Love.

One morning I was not feeling well and sat in the back of the Church building. I was amazed or aghast at the traffic and disturbance that goes on during a Worship Service. "The Devil At church" just seemed to write itself after that experience.

THE DEVIL AT CHURCH

Did I cause the devil to visit Church today?
Did he ride on my shoulder when I went astray?
When I sat there without raising my voice in song,
Was he happy to see my face sad and forlorn?
Did he whisper in my ear causing me to talk?
Thereby disturbing others when I would be at fault?
Did he laugh gleefully as I sat unbelieving,
And did not follow the Scripture reading?
Was he smirking when for Bible Study I was not prepared?
And did he make me want to giggle and laugh out loud?
Did he urge me twice to get a drink of water?
Knowing full well It would cause some disorder.
Was he happy that I was being inattentive?
And becoming spiritually depletive.
I thought I felt him tickle me under the chin,
When for contribution only a dime I put in.
Fortunately, my conscience got me to thinking,
With heavy heart I began truth seeking.
I prayed to God to help me be better than ever before,
Triumphantly, I saw the devil slinking out the door!

In a Thursday morning Bible Class we were studying Ephesians I: In reading the lesson the teacher was asked to re-read verse 6, by Jim McCain, an Elder. When he had finished reading Jim remarked that verse 6 was especially touching in talking of "The Glory of His Grace" That phrase stayed with me the rest of the day and I read the chapter again and later the words to this poem was formed and written.

THE GLORY OF HIS GRACE

God's Love bestowed on us the Glory of His Grace
Which is promised through Jesus to all human race,
The Glory of His Grace gives us a choice
That glorious day we accept it, we can rejoice.
Blessings are ours when we trust and obey
By faith we can look forward to a brighter day.

Marvelous Grace that gives us peace,
Glorious Grace that will never cease.

When we walk in the Glory of His Grace,
We await the day we see Him face to face.
Let the Glory of His Grace shine in you,
Tell the world that Jesus' power is true.
The Glory of His Grace has made us strong,
Thus we sing this happy joyous song.

Marvelous Grace that gives us peace,
Glorious Grace that will never cease.

In 1999 I was asked to take charge of the Memorial at our National Association of Lively Families held in Augusta, Georgia. We always use the 23rd Psalm for most Memorials and to add a little variety to the Memorial, I wrote and read this version of "The Lord Is My Shepherd." I have also framed this poem and used it as a get well card for family and friends.

THE LORD IS MY SHEPHERD

Like a shepherd leads his wayward sheep
So does God lead me from sin so deep
I shall not want for anything more
For God's love is sufficient, I know.
In pastures of green I'm given rest
God has planned this for his blest.
He leads me by quiet waters still,
To satisfy my thirst by doing his will.
My soul is restored and made whole again,
And as his sheep I'm free from sin and pain.
Over the hills and through the valleys dim,
He leads me in all righteousness to follow him.
His rod and staff comfort me in times of stress,
I live to follow him and to do my very best.
He keeps me safe from my enemies and foes.
And with truth his almighty love he shows.
Therefore I fear no evil, from worldly travails,
His goodness and mercy for me will prevail.

I WILL DWELL IN THE HOUSE OF THE LORD
FOREVER.

"We Miss You" was written after a dear friend of mine couldn't attend the services for several weeks. I had cards made of this and have sent it out to numerous Christians when they were not at the services. I hope and pray it has been an encouragement to all who received one.

WE MISS YOU

We miss you when you cannot attend
and with the Saints your voice blend,
at the Services of our Lord and Savior.

You miss the reading from His Holy Book
and remembering the Supper Disciples took,
at the Services of our Lord and Savior.

You miss hearing Saints offer up prayers
on your behalf as well as on ours,
at the Services of our Lord and Savior.

You miss communion with others
greetings from sisters and brothers,
at the Services of our Lord and Savior.

We pray that if you are ill
you will soon be up and well,
attending Services of our Lord and Savior.

TWILIGHT
REFLECTIONS
BITS AND PIECES

Life is what you make it as you go along. I feel that at any given stage of your life it can be and is the best. It just doesn't get any better. Then when the next phase comes along it is even better than the first, and so on, especially if God is the focus.

LIFE DOESN'T GET ANY BETTER THAN THIS

A hut, house, cottage or just a room
The haven of security you call home.
Deep in the valley or up in the hills
Trials and tribulations of overdue bills.
It's wonderful to be able to share
With someone whom you know will care.

LIFE DOESN'T GET ANY BETTER THAN THIS

A loved one with an unexpected kiss
The happiness of true marital bliss.

The joy of a newborn daughter or son
Watching them crawl, walk and then run.
Experiencing their first day of school
Teaching them to obey the Golden Rule.

LIFE DOESN'T GET ANY BETTER THAN THIS

The difficult years of chaotic teenage
Fads and haircuts that are all the rage.
Their excitement of learning to drive a car,
Then off to college or reaching for a star.
Seeing them through every emergency
Each and everyone of the utmost urgency.
LIFE DOESN'T GET ANY BETTER THAN THIS

The enjoyment of rocking a grandchild
The ecstasy of a beguiling smile.
Your parents reaching their last years
Recalling memories that keep you in tears.
Understanding that life does go on and on
confident a crown of Glory you have won.

LIFE DOESN'T GET ANY BETTER THAN THIS!

A GIFT

On Christmas Eve we did go,
viewing lights from door to door,
listening to chorales as they sing,
standing so sedately in the rain.

Happily we go heading back home,
to sit by the fire so toasty and warm,
opening presents under the tree,
with anticipation, first you, then me.

A gift in which I truly delight
a midget tape recorder that's just right
to record ideas as I lay sleepless in bed,
instead of sheep, they whirl around my head.

For me to record these thoughts is such a joy,
and to be able to use this incredible toy.
Thank you Dear, for being so kind,
now you can hear ideas that cross my mind.

BEAUTIFUL LIGHTS

Beautiful Christmas Lights!
On the darkest of nights,

Send a warming glow
Across the glistening snow.

They are heartwarming and cheerful!
Even to the most fearful,

Who for some peculiar reason,
Do not enjoy the Holiday Season.

To those who are in sorrow,
With no hope for tomorrow,

The lights emit a comforting glow,
That helps them JOY to restore.

I have used "Christmas Time" as my Christmas card, copying it on pretty computer paper and decorating the envelope with Christmas stamps.

CHRISTMAS TIME

Christmas is the time each year,
That brings greetings of good cheer.
A time for remembering many friends,
For New Year's resolutions to begin.

Each day often brings a new surprise,
Cards and gifts opened before our eyes.
It's a time of gladness and blissful joy,
As children gleefully try out a new toy.

Families gathering round the dining table,
Giving Thanks that they are still able
To enjoy each other's joy and laughter,
As the clatter resounds above the rafter.

The grandchildren enjoy the playful mirth,
From parents who, for once, forget the dearth,
And the awesome task of providing daily living,
Midst the joyous spirit of Holiday giving.

A NEW YEAR'S RESOLUTION

The Holidays are over and again we are alone,
happy that the folks are safely back at home.
The train, tree and trimmings carefully put away,
where in the attic another year they will stay.

A New Year's Resolution the "clutter" to organize,
as day by day it grows bigger before my eyes.
I start with magazines heaped in a pile,
scissors in hand, recipes I plan to file.

I scan articles, crafts, and a headline or two,
continue to work, trying hard to get through.
Here's yet another diet plan, I see,
but is it really one that's good for me?

Alas, a book-long novel I planned to read,
Oh well, it's not organizing but relaxation I need,
after a hard day at work before to bed I retire,
more enjoyable and much less effort does it require.

Putting scissors and file away for another year,
I start reading about exotic places far and near.
There won't be much organizing now, I fear,
but at least I can keep the "clutter" I hold dear.

My daughter loves to raise chickens. She has gotten chickens from many different people. This particular chicken she got from her Aunt Clara thus the chicken's name. She always names her chickens after someone or the place they came from. This old hen didn't like her husband. She always flew at him when he came any where near her. It was a mystery to us why she took such a dislike to him. Don't tell me chickens don't have a personality of their own.

AUNT CLARA

I don't know how her love to gain
Or why I cause her such pain.
Aunt Clara really hates the sight of me.
Screeching and squawking like a banshee.

With ruffled feathers she jumps on me,
Backing off she will start in again
Just like an old wet setting hen.
If I wasn't so scared, laughing I'd be,

Cause Aunt Clara is my pet chicken, you see!

There are several shady roads here in Marion County. It's always a joy to ride under the canopy of moss hanging trees.

A SHADY ROAD

In a tunnel of yellow jasmine,

strands of moss swaying in the wind,

under a canopy of mighty oaks,

the bright dappling sun spots,

like mystical dancing elves abound.

A vision of beauty, seldom found

on a winding, lonely country road.

covered wagons, a humble abode,

hidden by purple wisteria vines,

takes you back to the olden times.

I spent a week in Georgia during hunting season in a small mobile home listening to the rain beating on the tin roof of the porch. After several days the storm got heavier and stronger and the clouds angrier and angrier until the sun came out bright and clear and a gentle breeze blew the clouds away. The birds started chirping, feeding and singing and the butterflies fluttered about enjoying the fresh air.

CLOUDS

Soft, gentle wafting clouds
cotton white and fluffy
floating,
softly across the blue sky
lazily dancing, gliding by
slowly drifting
UP, UP AND AWAY!

Low, heavy hanging clouds
dismal, quiet and calm
soaking,
day after day, all week long
at last in creeps the sun

chasing them
UP, UP, AND AWAY!

Stormy, black thunderous clouds
snapping, snarling and vicious
roaring,
sending hail, lightening and wind
crashing down—and then
bouncing angrily
UP, UP AND AWAY!
After the clouds are gone
You wake one bright sunny morn,
To hear birds singing sweetly in trees,
Catch a whiff of early morning breeze,
See among flowers a beautiful butterfly.
Before it sails into a cloudless blue sky,
UP, UP AND AWAY!

I love the Florida weather, the warmth in winter and the breezes in the summertime. It is always refreshing to walk barefoot along the sandy coastline, feel the ocean breezes and smell the salt air.

FLORIDA'S SAND

Florida's Coastal Land

Beautiful White Sand

Clear Blue Waters

Mild Sunny Winters

Stately Palm Trees

Waving in Balmy Breeze.

We Wondered Why Natives Would Smile,

When we Say We're Only Here For Awhile.

"We Got Sand In Our Shoes"

For This Is The Place We Choose

Just As The Old-Timers Always Say

We Settled Here To Stay!
In Florida's Homeland

With Shoes Full Of Sand!

FLOWERS OF BEAUTY

SPRING IS A BEAUTIFUL TIME OF THE YEAR!

April Showers
Blooming Flowers
Birds Singing
Heart-bells Ringing

BROOKS BABBLING WITH WATER SPARKLING CLEAR

Wisteria swaying in the breeze
violets peaking among the leaves
Dogwood blooming all around
Greybeard hanging its fronds down

THE EYES BRIMMING WITH JOYOUS TEAR

Daffodils nodding yellow heads
Azaleas meshing pinks and reds
Pansies in a purple row
Amaryllis with iridescent glow

GOD'S GLORY SHINES IN EARTHY SPHERE

As a child living in Georgia I remember: the freezing cold of the winter,
hugging the fire and hating to have to go outside for another load of
wood, clay roads, icicles hanging from trees, a beautiful wonder land to
look at while in a warm house.

GEORGIA WINTERS

Georgia Winters are so cold,
the chill seeps
through no matter how warm you dress,
And make you feel so cold.

The sleet hangs from an evergreen tree,
in long icicles
and frozen paths
makes it hard
To stay upright and on your feet.

The wind blows keenly and bleak,
whipping around the house
in great gusts
pushing you back
Two steps for each one forward you take.

Snow rarely falls on the earth,
for snow cones
to hearten us
just dreary cold to
Make welcome a warm fire on the hearth.

Spring weather is just around
the corner promising
hope in a re-birth
with bright flowers
Pushing up from the thawing earth.

SEPTEMBER'S SONG

Crisp, cool, clear air covers early morn,
As a brisk breeze sweeps the fading dawn.
Morning doves coo as they twitter to and fro,
Picking up seed along the wild hedge row.

Sing 0' Sing September's Song!

Busy Squirrels happily hoard fallen nuts,
Pickers drag long sacks down dusty ruts.
Huge pumpkins turn orange in the farmer's field,
Pretty flowers fade when summer begins to yield.

Sing 0' Sing September's Song!

Clusters of goldenrod grow on a sloping hill,
Brown cattails adorn edges of the water mill.
Geese fly in Vee formation toward winter home,
Colorful wood ducks swim lazily on golden pond.

Sing 0' Sing September's Song!

Happy kids on a big yellow bus wave goodbye,
Mothers turn to fall cleaning with a sigh.
Glorious trees display leaves of vibrant color,
September's Song announce the close of Summer!

Sing 0' Sing September's Song!

SUMMER TIME

In the summertime on our small Georgia farm,
We never needed an alarm.
Red roosters started crowing at crack of dawn,
Followed by birds with their sweet song.

Milking cows mooing over sweeten grain,
We were anxious for our day to begin.
An 'ole fishing pole and worms in hand,
Down the long dusty lane we ran,

Warm sand squishing between bare toes,
Fresh morning scents tickling our nose.
Water rushing in clear bubbling brook,
Feet dangling we sat and baited our hook.

On a summer day so hot and sultry,
From time to time we grow thirsty.
Water from a sparkling cold spring,
Quinches thirst like nothing else can.

No clock to remind us of work duty,
Just time to enjoy nature's beauty.
Morning sun sparkling on grassy dew,
Spectacular skyline with an awesome view.

No other time would ever compare,
With the freedom we enjoyed there.
In the summertime on our small Georgia farm,
With all it's rural beauty and charm.

THE FOUR SEASONS

S pring is the time for spectacular renewals,
R eaching toward Heaven are the blooming trees
I nfusing the land with a sweet, soft breeze
N othing is more beautiful to see on earth
G laddening the heart with love, hope and birth.

S ummer is for relaxing, swimming and playing
U ntil school begins again in the fall
M any children with marbles, tops and ball
M ake the long, lazy days seem so short
E ven when they have some work of a sort
R emembering family visits, goodbyes and waving.

F all-ing are the varied leaves so beautiful
A long the banks of a babbling brook
L etting cool water run over the foot
L ots of time yet for raking and being dutiful.

W inter is the time to enjoy the snow
I nclosed in homes with fires aglow
N estling among the quilts for warmth
T aking time to Thank God for health
E ver conscious of His Hand in it all
R esting in faith of His Call.

One Thanksgiving my daughters, daughters-in-law and I all went shopping together. We had a ball, trying to outdo each other with the best sales and arrived home, tired but excited and proud of having done a good job of staying within our budgets.

HOLIDAY HUSTLE

The day after Thanksgiving early in the morn,
leaving family in beds so snug and warm,
off we go hurrying-scurrying around town,
east side, west side, all up and down,
to see what sales we could find. What a crowd!
Bargains of which we are so proud!

Off we go hurrying-scurrying to the mall,
carefully shopping, while having a ball.
Looking, talking, comparing prices, you see,
all for something special to put under the tree.
Here we go hurrying-scurrying down the hall
looking for a bargain, not just anything at all.

Enjoying the excitement and noise very much,
We are not finding items on our list as such,

Tired, hungry, and very, very broke,
We go hurrying-scurrying home to gloat,
with all our packages wrapped and not to be shown,
to little ones, big ones, anyone till Christmas morn.

Several years ago when my granddaughter Ashlynn was about eight years old she asked me to write a poem about Thanksgiving for her to read at a Church program. Keeping in mind that this was for children, I wanted to catch their attention thus the "beets" along with good things to eat. I felt it successful as I got many a "yucky" comment as a result.

THANKSGIVING

When the Pilgrims came over on the Mayflower ship,
They gave Cromwell's men the slip.
Freedom to worship was their goal,
Indians didn't stop them from planting the soil.
They toted water from the river spring,
Caught fish and hunted wild game,
They set aside a day to give Thanks for what they had grown,
For log cabins, kerosene lamps, straw beds, that they
were glad to call home.

**Their tables were laden with good things to eat,
Pumpkin pie, Turkey and dressing, Cranberry sauce,
Corn and even some beets!**

Today we have much more to be thankful for,
Many things the Pilgrims never heard of or saw.
Cars, motorcycles, trains, planes and trucks,
television, Videos, Stereos and such.
We still observe the day they set aside for Thanksgiving,
With families and friends together re-living,
The tradition started years ago by our fore fathers,
Who gave Thanks for blessings received from God our Father.

Our tables are laden with good things to eat,
Pumpkin pie, Turkey and dressing, Cranberry sauce,
Corn and even some beets!

HAPPY ANNIVERSARY

WMOP is on the air celebrating it's 40th year,
Always playing music pleasing to Country's ear.
Marty Robbins, George Jones, and Roy Acuff,
Those Williams' Boys—one is not enough!
Remember, about 20 years ago, Country Jim
Kept listeners enchanted with his wisdom,
And the working people tooted as they passed by,
Getting a greeting when they caught his eye.
Remember Tony and Hack with their morning prattle,
Making it more enjoyable to enter the work battle.
We enjoyed John and Ken giving out helpful hints,
To motorists on the rules of Florida's driving limits.
But Ole' Country Jim really hit the jackpot,
When he found Ms. Scotty to fill her spot.
WMOP now gives us the fifty-fifty mix,
Day after day from nine till long after six.
Keep up the good work and we'll keep listening,
Richard with news, Ben, Wes with music a' mixing.
Thanks to WMOP for forty pleasant years,
When we have to say goodbye it will be with tears.

HOW CAN KIDS RAISED IN THE SAME FAMILY BE SO DIFFERENT

That question has been asked time and time again,
The answer you get may not be one and the same.
How do other siblings affect the formative years,
What about their association with teenage peers?

Does the parents verbal communication,
Along with school and church dissemination,
Determine how one child will accept and understand,
When another will reject and make demand?

The rules, regulations, discipline, order and administration,
Are loving methods of instruction, education, and preparation,
To insure that the child's character, nature, and personality,
Will help build stability against tribulation and adversity.

How do we help children who are in an endangered situation?
CARE enough to listen to their cries of discontent and frustration.
Let them know that God cares and will keep them from all harm,
While holding then close, safe and secure in loving arms.

If they will only to God turn
Accept Him and be willing to learn
That He is the calm in the night, an anchor in a storm
To keep them protected, snug and warm.

LOVE

With lamplight dimly glowing,
love talk softly flowing,
Eyes shining so bright,
the future seems so right,
As she gladly accepts his ring
Making him feel as a royal king,
Love light
In their eyes shining,
of dreams with a silver lining.

I wrote "The Precious Children" after observing my great-granddaughter playing. Her inquisitiveness, nimble fingers and alert mind were so exciting to watch. Children at this age are so precious, at a learning stage that gives us hope, that all will be right with the world.

THE PRECIOUS CHILDREN

Precious little children are delicate and so sensitive,
Happy, joyful, busy and very inquisitive,
Please don't say they are in the "terrible twos".
If you do you are the only one to lose.

To watch them explore you gain an education,
As they try out new areas with determination.

Little fingers can find the smallest crumb.
As their minds seek to find, discover, and learn.

Little hands full of sticky, gummy goo,
Are so loving when they feel of you.
They stand so firmly on precious little feet,
Don't glance away for they are ever so fleet.

Darting out of sight in a moments time,
Feeling their freedom so very sublime.
You can almost see little wheels at work,
Behind those beautiful eyes a genius may lurk.
You never know what they will do next,
It doesn't matter of what race or sex,
For they all are very precious and dear,

Need loving care from those who are near.
We are responsible to help them grow
To be all they can be and much, much more.
Let's teach them good morals and laws,
Keep them from the devil's grasping jaws.
Help them to develop their bodies and mind,
Love them completely and honestly all the time.

I wrote "Surprizing Behavior" about the time President Clinton was being inaugurated as President of the United States. At that time, I was reading a Gothic novel describing in detail the dress of that period and also had an occasion to observe a nervous waiter being trained. It all seem to come together in a poem. This is Angie's favorite.

SURPRISING BEHAVIOR

A formal party was given for the President
invited were all the upper class residents.
The men attended in black tie and tails,
coiffured hair and well manicured nails.
The ladies in silks, satins and pearls,

perfumed and powdered with lacquered curls.
To everyone it appeared to be a success,
but not so to one particular charming guest.
A gracious lady with hair of spun gold,
was aghast at the lack of manners, I'm told.
When her "No Thank You, perhaps later",
surprised and startled the attending waiter
into dropping the refreshment platter,
she said "I'm sorry, it doesn't matter.
Kneeling, her "May I help clear this mess?"
was such a surprise to all the guests
that everyone got as quiet as mouse,
His "Thank You" was heard all over the house.
A lesson in humbleness was learned that night,
taught by an elegant, graceful lady who was polite.
Her "Please", "Thank You", and "May I help",
stood out in a crowd of distinction and wealth.

THANKS FOR THE MEMORIES

As I drive along the highway
Going to and from work each day. . . .

I see children playing jump rope or hopscotch,
riding bikes as the littlest ones sit and watch.
Some feeding bread scraps to ducks down at the lake,
while others gleeful glide to and fro as they skate.

Then as I pass the neighborhood country store,
yesteryear's memories flood my mind once more.
I see barefoot youngsters buying a loaf of bread,
perhaps a lollipop or Mom a spool of blue thread.

I glimpse a devoted wife with three happy kids
sitting under an oak tree, opening the lids
of mason jars and spreading a picnic lunch
for her hard-working husband and his bunch.

Riding along a friendly, back country road
I pass a log truck with an extra heavy load.
I see people picking fruit and being merry
as they anticipate a baked pie of blackberry.

Slowing down I travel a bumpy, dusty lane,
by fields waving with stalks of rustling cane.
An old lady sitting on a cottage porch shelling peas,

And enjoying the shade of spreading oak trees.

All these things and many, many more,
Bring back memories of days gone. . . . . . .

Books are a source of pleasure and comfort and can take you to many magical places.

THE LIBRARY

The library is a place of quiet peace,
Where from worries you can find release.
In browsing along shelves loaded with books,
You find many interesting subjects in the nooks.

For through the pages of many a book,
There were some enchanting trips I took.
Some were far away and some close to home,
But all of them where I chose to roam.

The library has been a source of joy and pleasure.
From school days to golden years of leisure.
It is now with delight that I applaud,
The library truly a place of reward.

We had built a home and lived in it for over thirty years. When I retired, we decided to move into the country near our youngest daughter. The move was certainly traumatic but we have adjusted well and enjoy being here under the oak trees, feeding squirrels and listening to the birds sing.

MOVING

Moving is such a traumatic and sad feeling
When we think of everything we are leaving.
A house built with hard work, care and love,
Filled with memories that make it a home.
A street where we know each curve and rock
Memories of good neighbors on each block.
Trees we planted as seedlings with great care,
A secure feeling of familiarity in the air.

However, our home is really found within
A special place for family and friends.
This we can take to our lovely new abode
That's near to loved ones—just down the road.
We are excited to have beautiful new curtains
And a change from our mundane rut for certain.
Planting and watching new seedlings sprout
Make it all worthwhile without a doubt.

At our National Association of Lively Families we always have a memorial for the members that have passed away during the year. I was asked to take charge of the memorial in 1997 and I wrote "Roses" and read it at the Friday evening meeting in Gatlinburg, Tennessee. I have copied this poem on pretty computer paper and used it as a sympathy card for friends and relatives.

ROSES

ROSES BLOOM AND ROSES FADE,
MEMORIES OF LOVED ONES ARE STAID.

LITTLE THINGS REMIND US EACH DAY
OF THOSE WHO HAVE GONE AWAY.

THE WORD OF GOD REMAINS TRUE,
HIS LOVE FOR US IS PURE.

SEPARATION IS ONLY FOR A SHORT TIME
MEMORIES REMAIN IN OUR HEARTS AND MIND.

TILL WE MEET AGAIN ON THAT GOLDEN SHORE
WHERE THE ROSES BLOOM FOREVERMORE.

We lost our brother Q.U. in April of 2000 and in August when the National Association of Lively Families met in Lynchburg Virginia I used "Precious Memories" for the Memorial along with the 23rd Psalm. I had written this poem after attending my brother's funeral and have since used it for sympathy cards for friends and other relatives.

PRECIOUS MEMORIES

Precious memories to have and hold,
Precious memories slowly unfold.
Memories of the one you hold dear,
Some fleeting, some so very clear.

Sometimes an unexpected thing,
A flower, a bird, the sound of rain.
The whistle of a passing train,
A rainbow in the sky, A yellow butterfly.
A walk down a dusty lane,
A stick used for a walking cane.
A hoe sitting idly by,
An eagle soaring way up high.

A word or special saying,
A loved one on bended knee praying.
A song praising God Above.
Exalting all men to love.
Roses of red, An empty bed.
A summer breeze, A sudden sneeze,
Many things bring to mind,
The loved one who was so kind.
These recollections and many more.

Are tributes held in store.
Precious memories to have and hold,
As shared memories slowly unfold,
Bringing comfort to the soul.

On several occasions of marriages, or wedding showers I have written a special poem for a special couple or lovely bride.

BEAUTIFUL MEMORIES

Beautiful memories are in the making
With each step down the aisle you are taking.

Memories of the first place you call home
For all the years hereafter to come.
Courage, faith and love it will take,
A bright future for you two to make.
With trust in God for your future plan,
Your love will grow and expand.

Through the years there will be much gladness,
Mingled with some tears and sadness.
Holding to your faith in God Above,
You will be blessed with an enduring love.
A love of grandeur and power sublime,
A love that will last through out your lifetime,

Beautiful memories are in the making,
As your vows to each other you are taking,

BEST WISHES ALWAYS

WAKE UP! WAKE UP!

Cock A Doodle Doo ! Cock A Doodle Doo !
Wake Up! Wake Up! Get Going!
The rooster in the barn is crowing!

The sun in the sky is rising
Making rainbows on the horizon.
The grass is fresh with dew,
The day aglow with morning hue.

Cock A Doodle Doo ! Cock A Doodle Doo !
Wake Up! Wake Up!—Get Going !
The rooster says with his crowing!

The cows in the barn are lowing
Their bags with milk overflowing.
The horses and pigs need feeding.
The garden spot needs weeding.

Cock a doodle Doo ! Cock A Doodle Doo !
Wake Up! Wake Up!—Get Going!
The rooster continues his crowing!

The grass in the yard needs mowing
Mending in the basket needs sewing.
The fish in the pond are waiting
They only need a little baiting.

Now the rooster stops his crowing
His work is done for the morning.
God looks down on earth with a smile
He knows His creation is worthwhile.

"Walking the Line" was written after a day of hard work clearing out the boundary line between two plots of land in Georgia. When the children called to ask what we had been doing while at the hunt camp we couldn't help but rib them a bit.

WALKING THE LINE

A new meaning we stumbled upon today
For that trite old expression or cliché
Armed with an axe, machete and bug spray,
Down the border line we slowly cut our way.
Through dense woods and bramble vines,
We clear the way between two border lines.

Cutting, marking the line, then taking a bead,
We make our way through the tall, grassy reed.
Despite the scolding from angry blue jays above,
Through the brambles and briars a line we wove.
A startled frisky little rabbit hopped away,
Through the tall rustling grass, making it sway.

Pausing, we stretch, look all around to see,
A bushy-tailed squirrel standing looking at me.
Dropping his half-eaten acorn away he scampers,
As under the huge spreading oak limbs we hamper.
Eating a sandwich and drinking cold ice tea,
Relaxing in the shade of the gnarled old tree.

In the stillness, a Holy Presence we feel,
We stand in awe of God who made the world real.
As the bright sun glows in beautiful blue skies,
God's powerful love unfolds before our eyes.
For all us lowly creatures to enjoy for awhile,
Till we come to life's last lonely mile.

At the end of the day we completed our task,
Having cleared the right-of-way at last.
Happy and bone-weary we head for home,
Satisfied with a back-breaking job well done.
The kids called, "What did you do today"?
"Walk the Line", with a silly smirk, we say!

WHO AM I?

Am I a kind person with a gentle smile
One who for another will go the extra mile?
Do I give my word and keep it as though a bond
Or do I without regard use a lie to respond?
Do I turn away anger with a gentle word,
Or do I, scream until I'm heard?
Do I listen to risque jokes and petty talk,
Or do I turn my back and take a long walk?
In traffic, do I shake my fist and shout,
At the ones who often dart in and out,
Or do I calmly keep myself in line,
In spite of drivers who toy with my mind?
Am I the grouch who in the grocery store,
Is annoyed because the cashier is slow?
Do I patiently and politely wait in line,
when others ahead of me seem to waste time.
For the sick and lonely do I bake a cake,
Write a card or to the hospital a visit make?
Do I ignore my chance to do a good deed,
And to help the sick or those who are in need?
Am I a safe haven in time of storm,
One who is loving, kind, and warm,
A person who cares for my fellow man
Or one who just does as little as I can?
Who am I?

At our Poetry Club meeting we were shown a picture and asked to write a poem about it. I could envision a lost dog hiding in the bushes near a broken down house, waiting for his master to come home.

WHY DID YOU ABANDON ME?

Why did you leave me all alone
Without water or even a bone?
Did you grow too feeble and old,
Unable your own life to keep and hold.
Your old dog hiding in the trees,
among palm fronds rustling in the breeze.

Rusty iron nails,
Decaying wagon wheels,
Yard with overgrown weeds,
Spiders in webs spun,
Buzzing bees in the sun.

Ready at sign of danger to hide,
He turns his head to one side.
Listening, listening for that squeaky old gate,
Wondering what keeps you so late.
Always keeping watch over the home place,
Waiting, waiting to see your old wrinkled face.
Why did you abandon me?
Are you at peace, happy and free?

I was asked to write a poem for the New year's eve party of 1999 for some friends. As this was the end of one century and the beginning of another it would make history. A celebration of the beginning of a new century and the end of an old one. Always having God as my focus in all things especially the creating of His people regardless of the time era, I was able to write this.

BEGINNING AND ENDINGS

God created both the beginning and ending,
It's the "in-between" that needs our careful tending.
God controls all life beginning with physical birth,
During our growth and ending in death on His earth.
How we spend each day is what will count,
That God is the Creator we have no doubt.
When we celebrate this year's ending,
We anticipate the next one beginning.

The beginning of a day is beautiful to the eye,
Viewing the glorious sun as it rises in the sky.
The beginning of a month brings a fare of expense,
Often ending in a frugal search for a few extra cents.
At the end of each year there are taxes to be paid,
Beginning each new year resolutions are made.
The end of this Century brings a historic event,
The beginning of the next, great expectations are lent.

God controls all the endings and beginnings as he sees fit,
The middle for good or evil use, he gives us His permit.
Each and every day with goodness and love we can enjoy,
Or with bad temper, foul language and meanness destroy.

The end always comes with the setting of the sun,
In a golden blaze of glory upon the Western horizon.
When at last we come to this life's worldly end,
We want to spend it with Jesus, our Heavenly Friend.

Printed in the United States
3492